PIANO · VOCAL · GUITAR

# MERCYME
# THE CHRISTMAS SESSIONS

- 2   IT CAME UPON THE MIDNIGHT CLEAR
- 8   GLORIA
- 16   GOD REST YE MERRY GENTLEMEN
- 23   ROCKIN' AROUND THE CHRISTMAS TREE
- 29   CHRISTMAS TIME IS HERE
- 35   SILENT NIGHT
- 40   DRUMMER BOY
- 44   I HEARD THE BELLS
- 52   O HOLY NIGHT
- 60   JOSEPH'S LULLABY

ISBN-13: 978-1-4234-1261-8
ISBN-10: 1-4234-1261-3

HAL•LEONARD®
CORPORATION
7777 W. BLUEMOUND RD. P.O. BOX 13819 MILWAUKEE, WI 53213

For all works contained herein:
Unauthorized copying, arranging, adapting, recording or public performance is an infringement of copyright.
Infringers are liable under the law.

Visit Hal Leonard Online at
www.halleonard.com

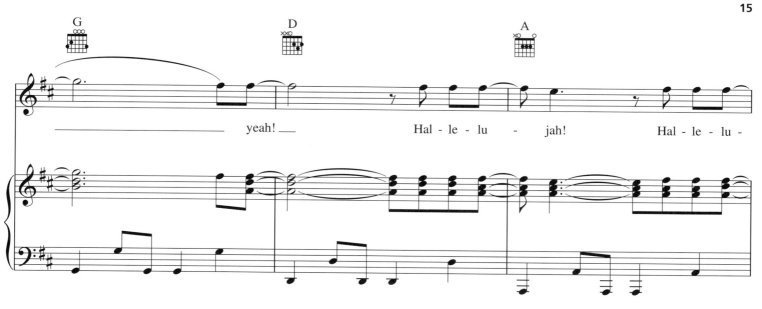

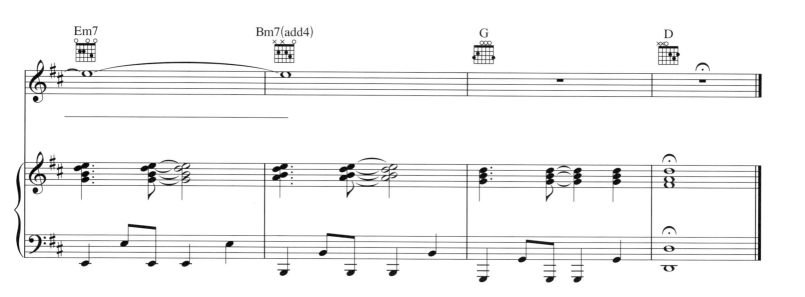

# GOD REST YE MERRY GENTLEMEN

Traditional
Arranged by BART MILLARD, MIKE SCHEUCHZER,
NATHAN COCHRAN, JIM BRYSON, ROBBY SHAFFER,
BARRY GRAUL and BROWN BANNISTER

© 2005 Simpleville Music, Wet As A Fish Music (both admin. by Simpleville Music, Inc.) and Banistuci Music (admin. by The Loving Company)
All Rights Reserved   Used by Permission

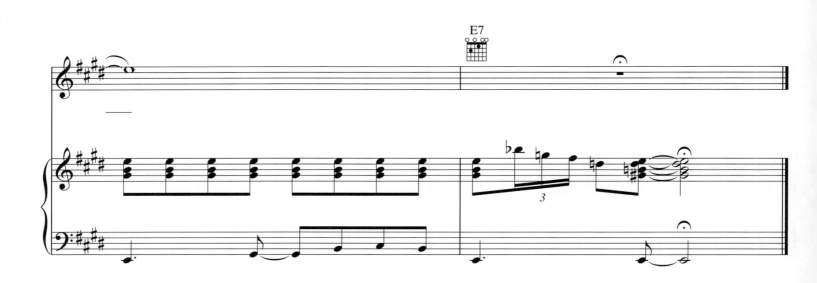

# Christmas Time Is Here

Words by LEE MENDELSON
Music by VINCE GUARALDI

Copyright © 1966 LEE MENDELSON FILM PRODUCTIONS, INC.
Copyright Renewed
International Copyright Secured  All Rights Reserved

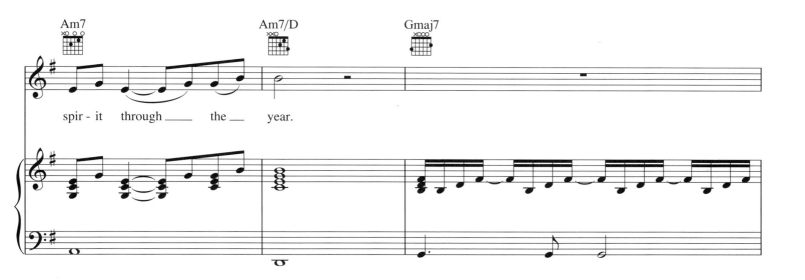

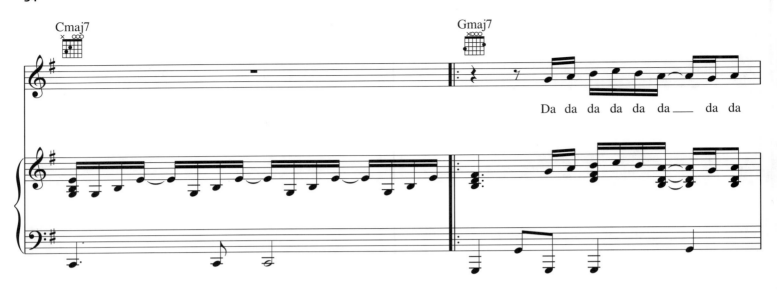

# SILENT NIGHT

Words and Music by JOSEPH MOHR and FRANZ GRUBER
Arranged by BART MILLARD, MIKE SCHEUCHZER,
NATHAN COCHRAN, JIM BRYSON,
ROBBY SHAFFER and BROWN BANNISTER

© 2005 Simpleville Music, Wet As A Fish Music (both admin. by Simpleville Music, Inc.) and Banistuci Music (admin. by The Loving Company)
All Rights Reserved   Used by Permission

# I HEARD THE BELLS

Words by HENRY WADSWORTH LONGFELLOW
Music by JOHN BAPTISTE CALKIN
Arranged by BART MILLARD, MIKE SCHEUCHZER,
NATHAN COCHRAN, ROBBY SHAFFER,
BARRY GRAUL and BROWN BANNISTER

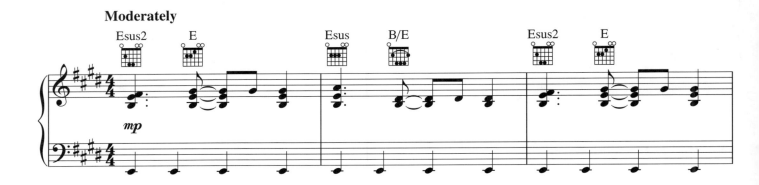
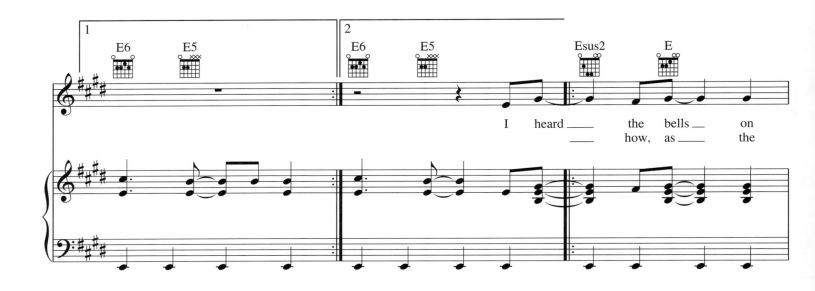
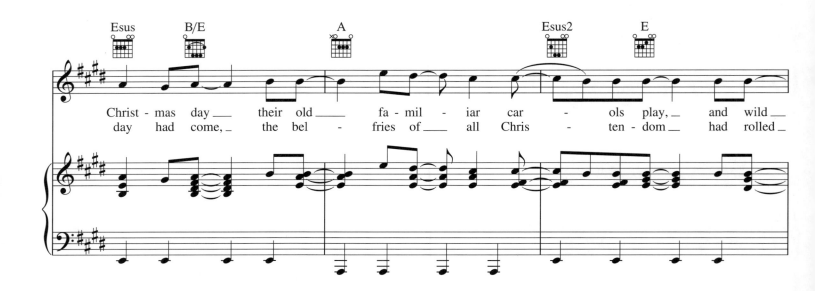

© 2005 Simpleville Music, Wet As A Fish Music (both admin. by Simpleville Music, Inc.) and Banistuci Music (admin. by The Loving Company)
All Rights Reserved    Used by Permission

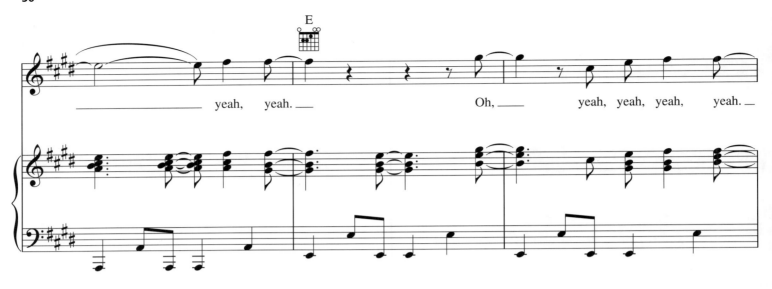

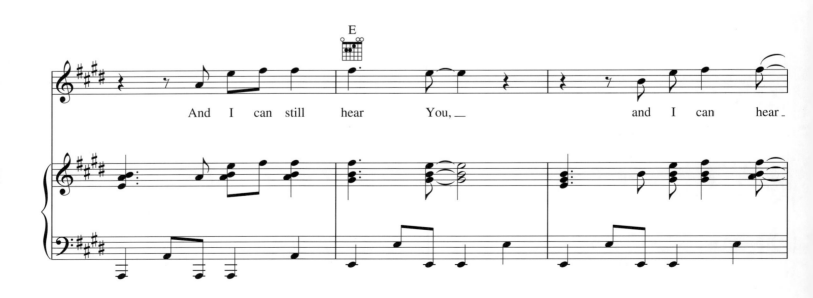

51

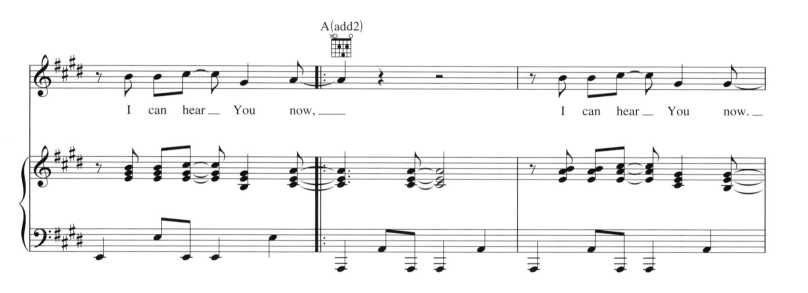
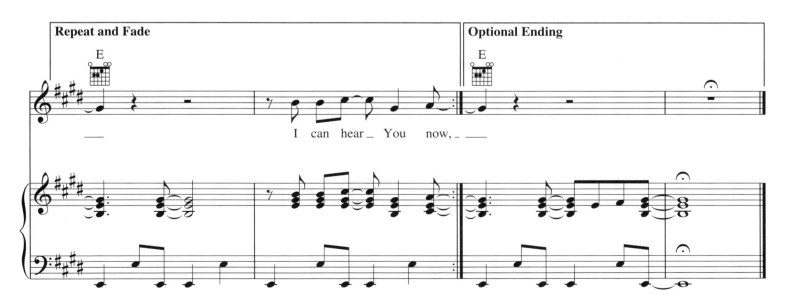

# JOSEPH'S LULLABY

Words and Music by BART MILLARD
and BROWN BANNISTER

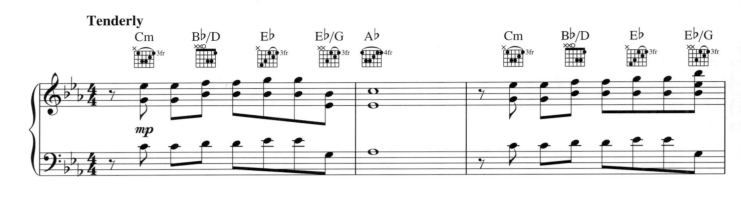
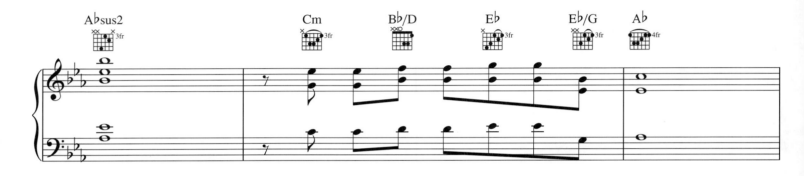
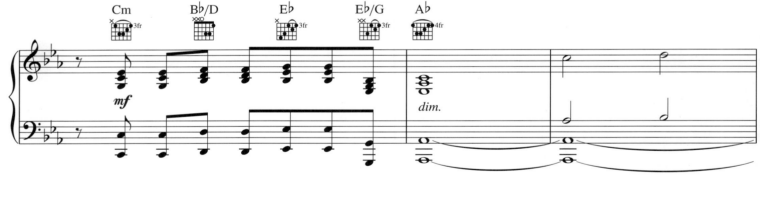
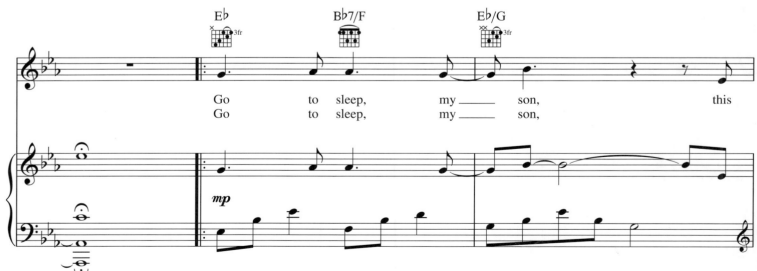

Go to sleep, my son, this
Go to sleep, my son,

© 2005 Simpleville Music (admin. by Simpleville Music, Inc.) and Banistuci Music (admin. by The Loving Company)
All Rights Reserved   Used by Permission